1 9 8 8

A GUIDE TO FORGETTING

Other books by Jeffrey Skinner

LATE STARS, Wesleyan University Press

THE NATIONAL POETRY SERIES

A GUIDE TO FORGETTING

Poems by Jeffrey Skinner

GRAYWOLF PRESS · SAINT PAUL

ACKNOWLEDGMENTS
Some of these poems first appeared, or are forthcoming, in the following magazines:

The Atlantic Monthly: "Prayer to Sparrow in Two Seasons"

The Cincinnati Poetry Review: from "Sonnets to My Daughters Twenty Years in the Future": "In the news today, a woman in fatigues," "What I want is deep connection, down to the task"

Commonweal: "Prayer to Cottonmouth Blocking the Road to the Pond," "The Maple Keys"

The Hampden-Sydney Poetry Review: "Pastoral," "Summer Guests"

The Iowa Review: "Happy Hour with Grady," "On a Bad Painting in the Lobby of IBM International," "Beauty and the Spider," "Prayer to Wasp on the Occasion of Its Execution," "A Grace," "Looking at a Photograph of My Father at My Age"

The Nation: "A Guide to Forgetting"

The New Yorker: "Prayer to Owl Hiding in Daylight"

The Paris Review: "Self-Portrait"

Poetry: "Hey Nineteen"

The Reaper: "Uncle Joe", "Love Notwithstanding"

The Texas Review: "Rescuing the Angel"

The author also wishes to thank the Ingram Merrill Foundation, the Corporation of Yaddo, and Bill and Gail Gorham for generous support which made the writing of many of these poems possible.

Publication of this volume is made possible in part by contributions to Graywolf Press from many generous individuals, foundations and corporations. Graywolf is a member agency of United Arts.

ISBN 1-55597-108-3
Library of Congress Catalog Card Number 87-83085
CIP Data on last printed page.
First Printing, 1988
9 8 7 6 5 4 3 2
Published by GRAYWOLF PRESS
Post Office Box 75006
Saint Paul, Minnesota 55175

THE NATIONAL POETRY SERIES

The National Poetry Series was established in 1978 to publish five collections of poetry annually through five participating publishers. The manuscripts are selected by five poets of national reputation. Publication is funded by James A. Michener, Edward J. Piszek, the Copernicus Society of America, The National Endowment for the Arts, The Friends of the National Poetry Series, and the five publishers—E.P. Dutton, Graywolf Press, William Morrow & Co., Persea Books, and the University of Illinois Press.

THE SINGING UNDERNEATH
Jeffrey Harrison
Selected by James Merrill/E.P. Dutton & Company

THE GOOD THIEF
Marie Howe
Selected by Margaret Atwood/Persea Books

THE HAND OF GOD AND A FEW BRIGHT FLOWERS
William Olsen
Selected by David Wagoner/University of Illinois Press

A GUIDE TO FORGETTING
Jeffrey Skinner
Selected by Tess Gallagher/Graywolf Press

NEW MATH
Leigh Cole Swensen
Selected by Michael Palmer/William Morrow & Company

Table of Contents

FOR LAURA AND BONNIE

FOR SARAH

"As I write down my thought it sometimes escapes me, but that reminds me of my weakness, which I am always forgetting, and teaches me as much as my forgotten thought, for I care only about knowing that I am nothing."

—PENSÉES, 372

ANIMAL AND OTHER PRAYERS

Trees and animals have no problem. God makes them what they are without consulting them, and they are perfectly satisfied.

With us it is different.

—Thomas Merton

Prayer to Owl Hiding in Daylight

Zealot in the trees, hot tiny speck
glowing in the dark of God's endless palm,
forgive me my absences! The clinically depressed
tenements of Bridgeport
ejected me into this calm, and now
there is too much rain, the leaves are pleading,
the green runs. All day, invisibly, you take notes,
like a businessman writing a novel
on his time off, a pale blue spark
snapping between your ears.
When will you visit? We desire visitations
but lack discipline to call them
on, and only our best shoes are shining.
I want claw, want your gold
headlights, your roomy coat of feathers.
I want to sleep days and work nights,
praising silence in high branches.
I want the microtonics of steel
drained from my blood. Oh the eclipse
has come and gone: show yourself.
You'll find my true love and me dreaming
on each other's shoulders, as the baby
breathes out tiny flowers in her crib
and the war continues, silently, elsewhere.

A Grace

Let's have no more *I remember*
poems, at least not until the self thaws out
and we can move easily in more than one direction.
So much lunatic pruning in a dead garden,

so much pretty blue smoke and mirrors. . . .
And let's have no more kneeling
for good reasons, dropping God's name
like a cast-iron doorstop,

forcing Him into the shape of a tree,
say, which would much rather go on treeing.
Let's sit down at the table, and eat.
Pass the chicken, sautéd with onions,

pass the broccoli, its green aroma
curling from the plate. Pass the boiled
red potatoes that slice open
with warm sighs. Pass the spring

water and the wine, the butter and the pepper.
Quiet the children according to their
needs. Quiet the radio and TV, all appliances
of confusion, of *I will never solve these*

too-painful and unending sorrows. Quiet
your opposite, as well as he or she
may be comforted. Quiet, quiet your own famished
heart. Let us fill ourselves in silence.

Prayer to Sparrow in Two Seasons

Little tongue-click, beggar at the redwood table,
how is it your fall makes so deep an impression
in the book black as loam, and as fragrant?

Song as warning becomes you, the sudden tilt
of your beak sounds like the first star coming on
one sweet May sky. There is a map through the trees

engraved in your skull—bone I could wear as a ring—
and your feet are black glass the serpent envies.
Once I held (Biology 101) your heart in my palm,

a tiny red clock, and asked for enlargement, life
bigger than life. This winter I pray only your
intercession, a handful of seeds flung over snow.

And watch as you peck the white crust, one eye
on my window, one for each seed, and nothing but God's
own poverty keeping you warm, keeping you.

What We Can See

"That confidence is no longer obtainable."
—Pound

And what did I, in the first place, swallow
unthinking? The painting of Christ surrounded

by children. His and their ease. Old man smoking and
rocking, *Ya ya, Jeffrey, ya ya.* Whispered Hochdeutsch.

Later the coffin in the living room, the great fact
of arms crossed over his chest. Blue vein in the temple

of the girl next door, so near the surface of her
white skin. Wine flooding the mouth, sweet, slow

solvent for the wafer. Smell of dead leaves
entering flannel, the pungent clean fires of autumn.

The boy with hemophilia who could not be touched.
The struggle to keep still, keep still and wait simply. . . .

Let's put salvation off until the next life, I said.
Let's agree sealed eyes are not trapdoors. Just eyes.

And the world is so delicate if you think about it
it collapses into memory. Or, what we can see—

desk, window, wall of trees and above it
all blue. A few hawks sliding off like words. . . .

Prayer to Wasp on the Occasion of Its Execution

You entered my face
like a whore's nails,
blew the skin out
red and dangerous
as a balloon
filled with gas.
Twelve years old,
I lurched
home, new pennies
slid from my jeans
ticking the side-
walk. Friends
dropped their mitts
and stared.
Only creature
I still kill,
prying your stucco
nests from rafters,
hearing the sound
of your body
breaking underfoot—
brittle, crushed
paper flower—
forgive this un-
redeemable
vengeance. Today
your descendant
enters through a hole

in the screen,
slow and fumbling,
falls off
the sill to my
desk. I will send
him back to God
using the sonnets
of Frederick
Tuckerman, an old
favorite, sad
lush lines to a dead
wife. Please convey
my regrets
to the Absent One—
I have not loved
all, or enough
without words,
lies or poisoned
hesitations.
Have mercy on me.

Beauty and the Spider

Once women were the beginning and the end of it,
and why a man would rather paint than touch
such skin beyond me. This lasted much too long,
and with luck will continue. At least, the idea.

The beauty of children is beauty's illustration
of its constant hunger for new forms, new bodies—
condensation rising from a rail fence at dawn
as if the solid world were melting, as it is.

Every fall is beautiful! The sound of stiff
dry leaves skittering down the roof at the winds'
brusque urging; high thin sheet of cloud,
blues and whites shifting like tropical waters.

October. A spider has dropped a line to my hair.
I am connected to her tiny cave in the tree
by a long shining strand. Always eager to be bitten,
I turn my head slightly, and both worlds tremble.

Prayer to Cottonmouth
Blocking the Road to the Pond

You lie like a wet branch fallen in the dust.
No; we pull up short as you spot us

and coil quickly, a stack of trouble. Cool water
seemed a good idea as we sat on the lawn,

heat rising from the grass as if the earth
itself sighed in its hammock, and the clouds

laid fat and drowsy on the horizon. But I've
seen you move across the water's surface,

the sickening ease. . . . For you, the old curse
is no impediment; you traded evolution

for a piece of shade, the line of your journey
to the present thin, but clearing a wide

berth. Assassin of the lowlands, slide
your vessel of bad dreams out of our way:

though we have fallen together, your children
are lost in the high grass, thinking it paradise.

Problems

for Steve Haiman

One of the things we can do about them is nothing.
I mean, to hold the mind in a just embrace
until the nattering stops, that twenty-four-hour
talk-show station in our heads, or at least relents,
letting some music through. But this is difficult,
perhaps harder than our problems themselves,
and our best intentions are torn, or disassembled
piece by piece by that same nasal voice,
so full of good reason and logic. My cousin
left work after lunch, bought a rifle
and hiked into the Kentucky mountains,
drank a beer, and blew himself away. No note,
no warning to his wife, who knew he'd been
depressed—but this, of course, was something
quite different. This is a solution of sorts,
but if you care at all about the people who love
you, you have to consider the mess it makes
in them, and goes on making. I cried
two hours at the news, and hadn't seen the bastard
in fifteen years. Denial, like whiskey, can work,
especially if you drink or lie to yourself with
a positive view, knowing any life is somehow meant
for suffering, a thousand little rehearsals for death,
and we must be gentle with ourselves. These
methods, however, are sitting ducks for the gods
of excess, and the crazy numbness that follows
worse than the reason you started. Religion,
ah, religion! As Dorothy missed the Scarecrow

I think we miss you most of all. God is transient,
and though He wants badly for us to see through
His disguise, placing Himself constantly before us
in the course of every ordinary day, we are busy,
very very busy. What an effort it takes to love!
So much of the self in the way, like a building
that must be blasted to make the horizon visible.
Friends, mates, children may be problems
in their own way, but what else do we have, really,
what better opportunity? But now I am preaching,
when it is nearly time to be quiet. In another poem
I wrote "The master will not listen to our problems,"
and it was true, this guy who was clearly opened
said he would teach us, but wouldn't listen to any
crap about sad marriages or lousy jobs, or guilt,
desperation, fear, despair, etc. He had his reasons.

Prayer to Doe Confused on the Shoulder of the Merritt Parkway

I can't slow down, too much pressure
behind. . . . Your innocence of death
is maddening! But even if I stopped
and managed to approach (you stunned

as a lawn ornament), what could I say
or scream to be sure you spooked
in the right direction? You're hopeless
outside the forest—why so curious

now, at rush hour, so lost? Oh these
are my own pathetic questions, you
cannot bear them, with that spirit thin
and frail as your ankles, your mind

diminishing in my rear-view mirror.
Our cars are so full of death
and hurry I pray you awaken, turn back
to the shaggy sunlight, the leafy floor. . . .

I myself was blessed: arrived home
on time, wife and daughters unharmed;
guiltless, almost happy through the night.
Timid sister, I could not say why.

Early Music

We have heard it
cresting a hill before the mountains began.
Or was it on an island
so small we could not lie down
and, forced to hold each other
were quiet at last? Then the flute seemed not
so self-pitying, but
clean as a spoon, as love
before too much knowledge.
Those were days
of satin and jealousy, of rich meats
basting in rich shadow;
a cap with bells
and the fool beneath dancing with a limp.
We'd meet inside the garden's
scent, heavy as tapestry,
a huge moon pressed like God's face
against the clear
night sky. The centuries emptied
a band of our hearing,
and the lute and the hollow drum
wait now until our child
is gentled and fussed into dream.
Then I take your hand
as we dance in slow circles the size
of faith—
that candle in a stone room.

Prayer to Housefly in Winter

Thousands of eyes batter against cold glass,
not knowing the landscape you desire is death.
And when we find your body, the dried

invisible suckers of your feet splayed upward
(a bit of clutter on the sill), it will mean less
than a kinless bum found frozen

on Eighth Avenue, and filed in the morgue
with a minimum of paperwork. Such is the snowy
grandeur of human death! Oh I am too quick

myself, too haughty, too much the talent
of my own appetite: made flesh and bone in America.
I pray the patience of your hunger—

how it expands over our heads
as you, stuck to the ceiling, quiet as a speck,
watch the interminable movements of fork

to mouth; waiting like Noah till the clatter
dies, and you can descend, minister
to the rich minutiae of our leavings, and feed.

Rescuing the Angel

It is difficult because she is wedged
between two buildings and heavy, heavy as grief.
And the dander from her wings makes me sneeze.
Nevertheless I have promised, and the cords
of my neck stand out blue
under the moon. Everything has a blue
edge—the sharp plane of her cheek,
the gargoyles thrusting their grimaces into space,
the windshields of cars
far below. This is my night job, and if
I don't free her by morning I must return
the next night, and so on. I straddle two ledges,
get a firm grip under her arms
and lift, teeth clenched, exhaling. She never speaks.
I didn't know my sins were so much trouble.
I didn't know each place I left
had entered me, like food, like too many eyes.
I didn't know this work would fall
to me alone, judging from how slowly
childhood passed. And now there's a pink
stain in the Hudson, and I must redouble my efforts
before the city wakes, though she hasn't
budged. I don't want some executive to look up
and think *My, what an odd statue,* me straining
like a madman above the concrete wings.

Self-Portrait

A tiny blemish where the sun-
glasses touch his cheek. It will fade.
From the corner of each eye, uneven notches
flare like the tracings of a split positron;

under each lower lid a thumbprint
smudge, worse on humid days, as now.
The irises still good—kaleidoscopic
chips of cerulean, aqua, liony

gold all float near the pupil on white
seas, all pull to bring the world in clear.
The hair, dark swirls and flourishes
at twenty, envy of older women,

has calmed to gentle swells, though still
thick, holding tight under scalp or skull
the desire to grow again wildly.
The waist will not shrink for self-

love or money. The lips are out of style.
And the blemishes add up, like drops
of rain on a white-dust road.
But in his chest the aging circus

goes on wandering, the rings more complex—
one flyer on the verge of a quadruple,
the knifethrower nearly blind, his hand
guided now by outline, now by love only.

A Guide to Forgetting

Give me back the old attic.
—Lewis Thomas

What is not made of words
should go first: a boy's shadow
falling beside him as he falls,
stones so mixed in composition
they are smooth, nameless;
the baby's tongue, music. . . .
Next, turn to the elements,
beginning with your collection
of star charts. As they burn
you may watch the sky
darken like a city at night
when the power fails. Forget
the city and every wrong
it has done you. Drag down
the numbered files
of your losses and insults,
the heavy small-print volumes
of doubt. Store them
in a room you will never
revisit. Melt down the key.
Forget your body, limb by limb,
each strength, weakness,
leaving the brain for last.
It will resist. Language
is also difficult, but

patience—one by one the words
fall away, like feathers
from a dying bird. You may
be tempted to save a few
favorites—*pulley,* for
example, or *tangerine;*
pretend they are children,
let them go. Lastly, choose
one face above all others,
whose eyes you most wish to carry
into eternity. Scribble
it over with black crayon.
There. You should have nothing
left but a sleek desire,
frictionless, not a mote of dust
to impede it, powerful
enough to call God
out of His endless meeting
to sit down face to face,
get things straight
once and for all, forever.
Forget this desire.

AS THE WOMEN SLEEP

Hey Nineteen

My hands poured acid down the blue walls
of the pool, while the rich wife inside tended to
who knows what—her elegant miseries, her African
 violets—
and the man of the house shattered clay discs
crossing the sun. "Hey nineteen!" my partner Ed
called up from a hissing cloud, "Where's
yer mind?" I stopped pouring and his face
stuck up out of the mist, furious and sour
at thirty-five, half a life gone
to seasonal work and a wife who pushed
him away, even on good nights. That day
lasted all summer, and I stayed inside
myself, a boarder in my parents' house,
scrambling eggs in the kitchen while Mother
ripped through her mysteries in the den.
There was a lost love involved, naturally,
and an old grammar-school friend who
turned up one night with a zig-zag scar
down his cheek, and a baggie of good dope.
We climbed the reservoir fence at midnight,
sat by a doubled moon at the lake's shore
and talked like Chinese poets till dawn.
We agreed that rebirth gets tiresome, even
within one life, and that the brain
is sad and lonesome up in its tower,
connected to the mainland by cables only.
Vietnam was one senior year away, or Canada,

or Sweden; a savage tender marriage
five years away, and the idiot's discovery
that literature would not save me
ten years or more. But at nineteen you can work
without sleep, you can dream without sleep,
and I rode the pick-up to the next dry pool
in Greenwich strangely happy, Flaubert
tucked in my back pocket for reading on breaks
while Ed sat and smoked, staring at the rich man's
slate roof, the wavering aura of noon heat.

The Maple Keys

In their whirling descent they preach,
they say there is no future like death,
no kiss like the turned black soil
of lucky landing. Matched, veined wings
snapped apart, flew again from small
fingers: Hamburg, NY, 1959. We spun round,
arms out, sinking slowly in imitation.
Grandma sat peeling apples on the porch
swing, her quick eye measuring danger,
the zone between us and the street.
Grandpa, invisible as usual, pulled
weeds from the feet of staked raspberries
in the back garden. The sky bulged with
clouds the color of ashes, then blackened
over our game. And Jodie got hit
with the first big drop on the forehead,
went wailing up the porch steps, fell
into arms smelling of flour and apples—
Grandma. They went in. I watched
a line of hail chase the sun
down the street toward town, I put
out my hands and they filled with cold
marbles. Then sudden as the last day
of summer the air warmed, drops spattered
and broke in my hair. Grandma called
from a window, but I was deaf, I was
soaked with wonder. And I undressed
in the loud pour, too young to separate

my body from weather, ran to the drainage
trough now swollen with two rushing
feet of rain. I sat down among twigs
and leaves carried on the stream's back
as Grandma slammed the kitchen door,
came running on heavy legs, her umbrella
pulling her zig-zag, then inverting—
flying off like a black jonquil. She cursed,
yelled again but could not rescue
me from such happiness, the water cold
through my arms and legs, thousands
of winged seeds swirling around my chest.

Looking at a Photograph of My Father at My Age

The graying brushcut stands up like a warning:
this black and white face is square, lean
and dangerous. Seven years out of the FBI and he
still wears the SI trenchcoat. Hands in pockets,
cigarette in lips, one eye squinting at a curl
of smoke. . . . The posing is only partial—
Bogart never worked undercover vice in Harlem
or chased a racketeer down the frozen streets
of Buffalo. The flat cruelty of the mouth is real.

As my hunger for the tales was real, sometimes
outweighing a reticence trained in by Hoover
(whose scary pug face guarded the den wall),
and I'd get one bare-bones cops-and-robbers
before bed. How much I wanted those shoulders!
—Level and wide enough to hold my sister
and me, one to a side. He'd do kip-ups,
brandies, one-arm push-ups between flipping
hamburgers on our Levittown lawn, my friends
awed into quiet. This was about the time
I began to withdraw, amazed to find more love
for Kipling than hardball. Mixing my Gilbert
chemicals in the attic, stroking a wan guitar. . . .
I slip the photograph back under drafts of old
work, study my face in the bathroom mirror.
Enough resemblance to imagine us as brothers,

perhaps—the photograph the one to step in
when the reflection caused a fight in some bar.
Later, the reflection might compose a little some-
thing, a sweet poem, to smooth out the photograph's
wife. She'd be touchy, emotional, crisp shadow
to his strength. Mum guardian of his weakness.

Love Notwithstanding

Whether Randy killed the hooker or not
we can't know. In jail he found God
working in the library. Unpunctuated letters
reached us full of praise and hallelujahs.
My father'd call me to his office,
read the latest one out loud and ask
what I thought. I said nothing.
I remember Randy's eyes at family
gatherings, so unblinking and intense
I imagined them lidless, brimming
with the wrong current. Eyes that stared
me into corners. Mother jumped
each time he laughed, a rackety scale
coming out of nowhere. Out on parole
two years now and the gossip from Shreveport
says he's back inside the bottle
and spending like a sailor. Then the letter
we all knew would come, comes: Randy asks
four grand, to be paid back ten bucks
a week. "I'll be dead before I see it,"
the sane brother says, and signs the check.
Lawyers' fees, schooling for his kids,
the rent, the car, now this: lucky my father
can afford the invisible shift of genes. Lucky
a damned life can come so close, love
notwithstanding, and still not be our own.

Uncle Joe

Said he knew the farmer so we could shoot
in his fields. I don't know caliber but the gun
seemed taller than me. First round went well—I blew
the beer can off the stump. He said you're
okay, kid. But the next time I relaxed and the butt
slipped from my shoulder. That crack was louder,
the scope kicked back, cut a red half moon
in my forehead. Jesus, he said. I didn't know
until my hand came away sticky and wet. He swept
me up and ran to the farmhouse. The farmer's wife
wore an apron like the forties had never gone.
She cleaned the wound and pulled the skin
together with a white butterfly. Only
then did my fear break open. I cried like
an idiot. She said if that's the worst thing
ever happens to you you'll be the luckiest
little man on earth. The truck cab stayed quiet
on the way home, Joe probably thinking Christ,
Doris'll be ticked. I remember turning that woman
over in my head, her words. What was the rest
of my life that she could say such a thing so calmly?

Summer Guests

for Bill & Gail Gorham

They rinse their glasses in the sink,
they bring their own towels. "The water's so clear!"
Gail says, floating dangerously close to rushes
where the mad turtle lives. Always,

they are about to abandon the city,
or they are on their way to Turo on the Cape,
or they are thinking seriously about children. . . .
You and I form a middle ground,

our new child paddling across the linoleum
in her ball-bearing walker,
eager to claim her first share of troubles;
books we no longer need piled up like weights

in the attic. Morning cup in hand,
they wonder at the cow's quick gait
crossing our yard; comment on the floor's patina,
the pastel quilt; ask about possible ghosts

living thin lives in our walls. . . .
Whatever *we* say, they are all smiles.
And on clear nights we sink into lawnchairs
traveling slowly under the stars, and sip

cheap wine and try to speak lightly
of the life between visits (still baffling!),
accompanied now by a dark wind brushing the leaves.
Older, their smiles are deeper

set, the pattern of their gestures
perfected. When they leave
it is always Sunday, and the gravel spurts
from their tires, punching holes in the rhetoric

of goodbye. A thin scarf of dust
rises between us, we wave the baby's hand and they
wave back, until their smiles diminish
into tiny crescents slipping over the far hill.

The City Out of the Boy

Rainbows hang in the eddies
and the best spots are rubbed smooth by Old Tom's
wooden foot. Day to day I can't remember
the names of plants, *Jewelweed*
slips from its leaves with each new seeing,
and me allergic to poison ivy. "Nature
bores me," said Milosz, and I understand
how fast a landscape can be used up,
the pretty trees march off and leave you
facing the same old self. Joe says if you look
a long time in the stream things begin
to happen: larvae disguised as sticks,
Steelhead shadows. But I have these city eyes
and the water just goes by like traffic,
transparent car after car. They're talking
bloodwort and banana slug in the clearing
and I'm on the bridge with my feet
numbed by the stream and thinking
of a Stamford woman who found a tree
with her Toyota at sixty-plus. It was rainy
and dark and you know how the mists
can erase the shoulders of the Merritt
Parkway, the sudden curves, the tendency
to sleep, etc. We weren't talking at the time.
Her eyes were green as moss, her best feature.
Yes, yes, something is moving in the water!
But I can't name it.

To My Unborn

In our ignorance of each other
we are equal, though you begin
closer to all I have forgotten.
And I make no great claims
for this world—it will seem
too bright, noisy and full
of vague movements. This
changes little. Everything
else does change, however,
constantly and in all
directions, something
you should know about. Lucky
child! Your mother and I
are in love, you were conceived
on a clear day. We went out-
side to find five white
egrets perched for the first
and last time in a tree
overlooking the pond. I could
not make this up—a sign.
Before you read, hear
or understand these words
there will be many
failures and lost toys.
In this area I am expert,
a reliable source. Otherwise
I know little, not even how
you chose us. . . . I imagine

you studying long strips of DNA
in the yellow light of
the world in between,
a sudden flash of recog-
nition, then your descent,
accompanied by five white egrets.
Like little gods your mother
and I have prepared
a place for you, and will
welcome you with blankets, huge
hands and smiles that may be
tired, but also real, ancient.

Three Seas

The first sea is a formal invention
not without flaw—the glitter, say, sometimes too much
for human eyes, especially if the loss is recent.
But dolphins love the variations,
stitching the pleats of wave all morning
or all night when their bodies turn to blue
porcelain. I sit drinking with the ragged cats
of Portofino, as the billionaire's yachts
ride still as icebergs in the harbor, each with
its warm figurehead: tan blond in a bikini
polishing the brass. That was one sea.
Another took me under like a lip
too long, too long until my heart got stubborn
and I surfaced like a careless word,
rode a wave back to my parents on Jones Beach.
That was a childish sea, long and spiteful.
I pulled a hard and shining body from that water.
My own children bob in the third, their squeals
like scratches on glass. They don't know
how much the sea wants us back
so I watch them, shielding my eyes. They
don't know about the mirror on the ocean floor
I saw once and turned from. Or how many
others have gone down for a closer
look, their faces enlarging, kissing themselves
asleep, in the salt bed, the fourth sea.

For Chris, Sweeping

The brisk, efficient strokes
are no matter of necessity—
the few crumbs there could wait
or be forgotten. Half a world
away a Zen monk rises at four a.m.
to meditate two hours, then chews
mindlessly his small portion
of pickles and rice. Setting aside
a few grains to put back,
he takes up bucket and brush
to scrub the toilet. How
cleanly the morning sun
gleams on porcelain! Such work
goes on so far from our own
fractious lives, I can merely
dream it here. Chris, I am tired
of the need to fill our poems
with objects—the Mobil stations,
the strictly named flowers,
the knives and cracked doll-faces
that must appear each line;
I am tired of the absence
they point to. On a cold and humid
day the coffee I rise to
lets off its little sigh of steam.
Walking through the kitchen

I feel my bare soles pick up
tiny crumbs, and remember
that's the reason you gave
for sweeping: you wanted to walk
without accumulation, you wanted
at least that thin strip of your life
clean, free of complication.

I Close My Eyes

I close my eyes and lean into the sun.
Blood-colored tracings expand and contract.
Nearby a man shovels gravel, a sound
like the slow steps of a blind giant.

I don't know why I am here rather
than some other place, anyplace.
I beg the question, I hang my empty
head like the butcher's striped awning.

On a dusty road I smell rain.
A long way back details glisten, a room
full of women who can say goodbye
in seventeen languages, a rough sea.

And for years I've been trying
to adopt the word *quay,* but oh the red
tape! Still forest, I hear cells dividing. . . .
Let's calm down and reason this

out—if I could immediately
and fully admit my vast, my iron ignorance
would the world disappear? Or—heart,
you've gotten and lost and gotten

what you wanted, when will you quiet?
Under the little drum-set of moon and stars
I worshipped the dark, and the trees
held out their hands, and I did not return.

Pastoral

White breast to receive mistakes,
a dry field for the rain.
Even when you look closely
into the farmer's eyes
he is shielding the herd,
he is hating crow.

Dove: shadow of crow
unless the mirror's mistaken.
Noon light dapples the herd,
bulls play before rain.
The daisy's myopic eye
opens at dawn and closes

as the thick light closes
down in the fields. Crow's
young, hidden from the farmer's eye,
screech out his mistakes
in the high branch, in the rain.
The farmer will herd

a calf into the herd
out of love, to be close,
warm as leather in the rain.
But how in hell do crows
learn, so fast, my mistakes,
thinks the farmer as he eyes

them pecking scarecrow eyes
and dropping buttons on the herd.
A dove here is mistaken
should it even come close
to the coven of crow—
such a white breast would rain

blood and rot in this rain,
bring tears to the farmer's eyes,
salt his rage for crow.
Low clouds blanket the herd
and, nervous, they brush close
to the electric fence, a mistake

beyond mistakes in the rain.
The farmer closes his eyes.
As the herd sizzles, crow laughs.

On Repeated Failures to Understand Relativity

for Dick Allen

One hand rocking the cradle of little Hans Albert
as the other scribbles notes for the Special
Theory, a fat cigar glowing like a red star
from a mouth in the middle—exalted image!
I don't get it. Lost the moment the train leaves
the station, or a bunch of keys floats next
to the startled passenger of an elevator falling
at terrific speed, I close the book and dream
of Newton's apple, decomposing in the quiet grass.
The curvature of space is somehow easier—
I can see parallel lines converge, starlight
returning home, frail and weakened by its journey.
And the huge eyes, forever moist, deepened
less by failed marriages, less by death camps
and leveled cities, than by his own firm, flat *No*
to chance. Even as the instruments sharpened,
piling their evidence. Even as electrons jumped
their tiny rails beyond the odds. Even as death
itself reached in, releasing that astounding energy.

The Good Story

for Raymond Carver

The story was so right he wouldn't leave it
for fear the words might go on unreeling
in his absence and when he returned the story
would be over, the pages blank. *I should hit*
the john, he thought, and went on with his reading.
It concerned the death of a child
and what happened to the parents for three
days following the death. The man reading
the story felt each needle of its language and event
flowing out inseparable, even though a TV
issued spiky voices from another room, and the draft
of a ceiling fan made his hands
uncomfortably cold. The urge to urinate grew
as the story lifted bandages of random pain
from his own life, and he squirmed in his chair, angry
he could not hold the parent's grief
outside himself, or even stop reading.
Someone turned the TV up and he cursed and kept on
reading. The cold in his hands passed through unbearable
to numbness and he kept on reading. The need
to piss was so intense he had to clamp
himself through his jeans and hold the book
with one hand to go on reading. . . .
Gradually the man realized he had wasted
much, though not all of his life,

that his own sorrow was real and bound up in time;
that the child would not return miraculous
but leave the parents to go on after the story
ended. And the man kept reading, himself
invisible as music, until the last unsweetened word.

On a Bad Painting in the Lobby of IBM International

for Ray Mancini

The sly artist knew what he was doing—
all color and abstraction, no obsessive
rage. I sit with my red leather notebook
on my knee, waiting to enter the maze
of partitions, to sit and calmly answer
charges of substandard service leveled
by a blond manager with a gorgeous tie
and bright future. I will not defend
the sad imbecilities of my employees
but tack the blame on money, how slim
the margin of profit, how you get
what you pay for, etc., and he'll come back
with original agreements, the contract
is quite explicit on this point, etc.,
and we'll shake hands and I'll leave
carrying the implied threat of his smile
and a list of changes in personnel.
This is only the pattern of little whips
I get paid for (same as how many million
others?), and god knows I no longer blame
the pleasant receptionist who must ask
three questions one hundred times
a day, while she wants only to return
to the rating for sexual attraction
in *Redbook;* or the manager, doing his best
to rise, someday, he trembles to think,

to an enclosed office on mahogany row,
his service awards and aged brandy
hushed and elegant in the glass cabinet;
or the ones who believed TV promises
and now sit before terminals, pale green
light like a sigh on their faces;
or the guys trading numbers in the mailroom,
half joking, half praying for the combination
that might land them in the local paper,
one arm around a woman with an uncertain
smile; or even the strong-willed ones
who descend each noon from glassy clouds,
the ones who've learned to say three things
at once without anger and appear kind,
showing their even teeth—for some are
kind, and not one of them unnatural.
My client keeps me waiting. I light a third
cigarette, check my watch. The painting
on the lobby wall is right before me, calm,
easy to look at, so little movement inside
it is impossible to describe. I touch
my forehead and my fingers smear a thin
line of moisture. The receptionist is waving.

Happy Hour with Leary

In the middle of distant conversation
Leary winks and lifts his Chivas
and a tiredness settles into his voice.
For once I am fully there,
listening. He talks about the sea,
his tour with the Merchant Marines;
he remembers the money hidden
in his sock, and the late-watch—
looking at city lights
wavering on the black water.
He explains how his wife
was a good mother, attentive
to the details of comfort,
intelligent and fair, but how
whatever once held the center
dropped away the minute
their son kept silent in his room,
their daughter flew off
to school. And his wife
would not say what she wanted
and he could not guess or, later,
care. He had drifted
into his work—Facilities
Management, a section so forgotten
by the big boys that the house
in Greenwich had to go
and he moved into a decent,

bleak four-room condo in Stamford.
He was not unhappy: *What good's*
ambition, he said, *ambitious for*
what? He had his books,
real ones, and could afford
the theater once a month,
a Day Sailor harbored in the Cove,
the best scotch. Then he paused,
wiped his mouth with his hand,
leaned back in his chair. He ordered
another drink and toasted
my new family, my new book,
continued success! . . . *Ireland,*
he leaned in and whispered,
that's where I breathed
easy. . . . His grandfather lifting a colt
at eighty, sneaking shots in the
shadows of the feed room. . . . He went on
from there in a small voice,
and good, I thought, it's
good to hear, to see a man *speak*
in the lean heart of the business
day. The waitress brought our check
on a black tray with two foil-
wrapped mints. Leary opened one
with small pale hands and chewed
as he continued—
he was back at the sea, trying
to explain precisely how it felt
to approach the port of Oslo in May,
seventeen years old, not even the need
to shave yet every morning. . . .

The Last Poem to His First Wife

Sometimes, when I wake up tired, I think
of your hand coming from the back seat
to slap my face, in our own car,
in front of our friends. They sat there
like thick, unread novels.
And then I want those years back in my body.
I want the silly mustache I grew in defense
erased from the photographs, whatever
boxes they moulder in. I want
the walls I punched through replastered,
and all the dark little hopes I kept from you
hammered out like bent nails.
I want the nothing I wanted from you
and the universe you wanted from me
to mix and dissolve, once and
for all. Lifted by mercy, we have fallen
into other lives, you to a black-haired child
and a husband who works with his hands,
I to a woman no different than
my soul, two daughters God Himself sighs over.
I forgive you now, Elizabeth, I forgive us both—
that sad young couple wrong for each other
as salt and rain. I let go, here and forever,
the grief we shared, calling it love.

As the Women Sleep

A small window
holds a fan to pull out smoke.
Stars blink
between the blades.
Very late to be drinking.

Because I want it to
the room stays light. Ghosts—
less romantic, sad
endings, than recurring
middles. How much the page

longs for emptiness!
I lie about everything.
I am sometimes
entirely accurate,
clear as rain on a leaf.

My daughter's necklace
of plastic
charms lies twisted
on the floor;
many colors, cheap, pretty. . . .

You step from childhood
hoping the isolation

dissolves, find it
the one indestructible
thing you own.

Doubt is my only hope,
the strength of it.

SONNETS TO MY DAUGHTERS TWENTY YEARS IN THE FUTURE

Like a person hard pressed in an argument we shift the ground to our children & begin the defense of life all over.

—Robert Frost
Notebooks

¶

I wanted a boy, of course, wanted to create
in my own image, ambitious little god that I am.
But the long years spent chasing women immoderate-
ly stacked karma: now I'm surrounded by them.
Human flowers, your natural smell intoxicates
and the fine blond hair I smooth, reading books,
consoling a fall. My own boyhood aches
in me still, burnished wind of summer dusks
comes back: bike-riding through dinner, stickball,
mumblypeg in the marvelous junkyard; running,
running the long dark length of Grandma's hall
to leap her scented quilt. . . . Oh I've lost nothing,
and need no small version of myself to keep
boy pleasures. A daughter takes a farther reach.

¶

This odd-shaped head I've passed on to you both
signifies some equally odd sort of dominance.
At least, I tease your mother thus: the family myth.
Better, I suppose, than accepting dumb chance
has made us wrong for any hat in this world.
But body proportions are a great concern
all down childhood, and the precise way a curl
falls over an eye demands long, stern
concentration in the bathroom mirror.
Lucky time renders this vanity laughable,
and gradually our face becomes a comfortable blur
tended once daily, and forgotten. Odd skull,
blunt nose, unbeautiful feet, etc., come to mean
little. One wants a glimpse behind the screen.

¶

In the news today, a woman in fatigues
let loose an automatic rifle in a shopping mall.
Three dead, seven wounded. By now you'll
know, have seen a thousand images of disease,
cruelty, death in rags and formal dress,
failed negotiations, husband, child, wife beatings—
the endless catalog of humans who've so lost
the way, they tease evil in, thinking it unboring.
It is boring. Weil, Merton, a few others
were right—good is the only real surprise.
Do you love movies? I do, especially comedies.
One favorite moment: a bum in a Marx Brothers
film asks for a dime to buy a cup of coffee.
Harpo opens his coat, pulls out a cup, steaming.

¶

Books: your mother and I contentedly obsessed
with them, a fact surely evident. But
given all popular obsessions, not the worst.
And if, worse luck, it happens to afflict
you, may you at least stumble on real ones,
the kind that hurt and heal together.
It's not sentimental to believe pain opens
the way for love: I met your mother, fresh
from her own mother's death, as I ached
away from a first marriage, both our hearts
raw and leery. So it was wild, insanity
to hold each other our second night, so quickly
on the heels of separate griefs. The third week
I asked for children—it was right out of some book.

❡

Between my father and I, a vast language.
How can blood speak? He scares you even now
with his spiky eyebrows and his English apple
complexion, as he did me when I was your age.
—A man to trust from a safe distance, to allow
one kiss on parting. . . . Unlike a mother's pull,
oceanic, all dissolving and blind as salt,
father love must be content with small gesture—
a tree mutely offering its shade. Is that right?
In my father's back yard a gray wind lectures
the leaves, *fall, fall,* it says, and they do.
It is a kind of love. Autumn now, one week
left to write, unbroken, these small songs to you.
In my father's house, trying to make blood speak.

¶

No thoughts, simply the wind, the soft clatter
of leaves tapping their brothers as they fall. . . .
Last night at the Halloween bonfire
Laura, smudged clown make-up, improvised balloon
belt, took second prize for originality.
We beamed, pronounced it the first of many coups.
But you refused the ribbon! Then took it, gingerly.
I was proud of that. The people who'd refuse
any honor this world manufactures
could ride, comfortably spaced, in one elevator.
I myself keep a dirty book of acceptances
which I like to claim necessary for tax purposes.
I lie. The end of striving must be sweet—
riding down clear wind, naked as a leaf.

¶

Words rise and the sky accepts them, makes
no comment. Meanwhile theatrics below
fill up our calendar, fill in the daily blanks.
The news, that blunt instrument, chants *Now, now.*
Oh we can't be blamed for riding time,
which keeps dissolving us into someone else
before we get a chance to know our own minds—
not really. Incumbent world, closet of old selves,
what persists? If you answer greed too quickly
a wound opens in you like a pretty smile,
you make many friends and prosper. Say death
and disciples, artists, lovers keep you company.
Never say no, nothing, not in my life.
Say love and I and all the clocks go wild.

¶

Business feeds us. I never chose it, will leave
to teach, selling only myself. My first wife
said *Take your father's offer, now, or I leave.*
At the time I hated every corner of my life
and pain was the center, the only way to feel.
I took it. Seven years of paper money,
sadistic clients, employees who care as little
for their work as I, with less chance to get away. . . .
Your mother's heard me bitch like this
countless times, too many. Now I work for
her, and the two of you, the crap is easier
to take. Nothing noble: the common situation.
America, I know your heart! I'm in business—
claiming my share of the small, daily humiliation.

❡

For Larry King

As if to mime the expansion of the universe
our friends have moved away: Stuart to Charleston,
West Virginia; godparents Larry, Nina and Chris
to Boston. Gradually our field of affection
contracts to the four of us. We are not unhappy.
But I wonder how far this homeless trend
can continue—will we step into the next century
carrying a dozen wrong addresses for each friend?
Even Yeats could not imagine a center
so diffuse—he had all-homey Ireland. The melancholic
sap in me would find his way to discontent
in a Capra town, ringed by friends and lovers,
last scene a teary gathering. But each planet
hurts in its slow recession, no rest or cure for it.

¶

The way we came we back out of to begin again.
Crawling on hands and knees, no tolerance, a process
delicate and invisible as the formation of rain.
To an observer it looks like boredom: cloudy face
rummaging a horizon jagged with trees. . . . This is
as close as I can come to explain our writing,
the first and dreamy part, not only the moment we dis-
appear, pad in hand, to a room beyond your hearing.
Poetry never bought you a dress, or cured
an ear infection, loose tooth or bloodied knee;
never in fact cleared up the smallest mystery.
But you have to love a useless thing to find
its use, and love is shy of words. *Mindless song,*
the accurate ones mutter. We don't call them wrong.

¶

Sunday morning, rain, the prospect of all day
inside, the two of you at each other's throats,
your atonal chorus of demands. . . . Oh to walk away
once, simply! Forbidden desire! But history protects
you from your mother's and my worst selves—
we too had dutiful parents. What's passed on
in love, however much the giving of it severs
giver from his might-have-been, persists. So long,
languid mornings of fresh coffee and the *Times!*
So long forties flicks, prize fights in the after-
noon! My beer, my cheese and crackers! Goodbye
solitary walks, slow lovemaking with your mother. . . .
Hello, vast disorder with small hands and eyes—
Narcissus is dead, your first, most merciful crime.

¶

The snakes withdraw from unilateral dreams,
adding quick stripes to the intensity of green
foaming the lawn. All is alive, is summer.
Laura dances on a rock, legs bent by heat shimmer.
None of us can sleep through this humidity—
we twist in damp sheets and dream of watery
passages underground, firelight on wet walls.
Weathermen claim the flat milk-colored murals
the sky's been pressing down will lift;
two days. Meanwhile a floating irritation drifts
from room to room: sister cuffs sister, mommy
slams doors on daddy's expletives. Happi-
ness (never a stable kingdom) 's been overthrown.
We sulk inside our private body heats for rain.

¶

On a jet to Zurich, Bonnie cranky for a bottle,
Laura chattering to her dolls in the middle seat,
a swarthy guy stands up, wild-eyed in the aisle.
Sweat limns his hairline. He waves a thirty-eight.
This is the nightmare of final choices, no exit
and no moralizing on the op-ed page between
flesh of my flesh and the distillation of hate.
I will myself awake, struggle out of the dream. . . .
It's come to this, a parent forced to imagine
who he might save with a sudden movement,
which child or woman must die to save the others;
whether it's better to cower, holding tight. . . .
This world, pretty blue in your eyes, daughters,
also reels with the gunpowder smell of sin.

¶

Prayer is better left unspoken. Go to Eckhart
or *The Cloud of Unknowing* for reasons.
When the mind goes porous as the change of seasons,
push harder! Give up, suddenly, ideas of profit. . . .
Oh I am too much someone, too cluttered to instruct
you in such things. I can't shed my own evasions—
you scramble over my meditation cushions
and I don't say no. My faith is a fatty heart.
Try to find a man or woman who can die
when they have to, but think nothing of it
until the moment comes. They'll be clear-eyed,
lean, seriously witty, handy in a drunken fight.
In their presence you'll feel heavy and slow,
loud silence upending all you do and do not know.

¶

Sometimes I wish I could enter your sleep,
translucent and gold-glowing as the atmosphere
inside an egg. I would make no changes there
(not quiet the neuron storm when bad frogs leap
across the optic screen), even if I could.
I would lie down in the milk of young rest, and rest.
My adult dreams seem sometimes made of wood,
scaffolding for no building, unnecessarily complex.
Or—a dead lover, newly risen, faces me across
a room without doors, whining of her thirst.
I hold a shaky cup of water, certain it will spill
before I reach her with numb steps. Each loss
invents its own mythology, replaying scenes until
the screen dissolves into the sleep that lasts.

¶

Light figures the small grasses and flails
its shadow whips across the lawn. I see
this as you jump into my lap and I retrieve
my cigarette, an H-bomb fallen on ant hills.
This cooking out at dusk, so stubbornly American,
is the most of time I have to spend alone
with you, Laura. I entertain you as I can,
telling lame stories of princes and unicorns,
animating the trees. You exhaust and touch me.
Already the struggle for power is in you,
parent heart the hill, sister the opposing army.
You snatch her toys and block her way until
our voices rise like heat, pour down to scald you.
We watch your second birth, the crowning of will.

¶

The colorless cloud visits us from Chernobyl:
levels are up in all coastal towns. Safe,
they say, safe and graciously invisible,
drawing its pulsing veil without a whiff.
I don't know. There must be a pinpoint of sanity
somewhere, wisely unlisting its telephone,
feeding newsprint to a famished blaze. Must be. . . .
But what does it wear? Does it like to sit home
or go out dancing? Does it have kids? If so,
where does it hide them? From everything,
I mean. All this mess inside will have to be
cleaned up, like the toys threatening
our every move. And the janitor-elect probably
will be death, as usual: that man on the go.

¶

What I want is deep connection, down to the task
of shaving, or washing dishes. I do them, every
other night, but grudgingly, my impatient mind else-
where. This talent for absorption's easy
for you: when you run, you are just running;
when you cry, there *is* no greater sorrow.
How do we lose this knack, this gift for doing
each thing so fully the self steps aside; how
get it back? I've considered joining a monastery
where stillness is watered like some delicate plant,
but saw it was another lie, or would be for me—
better keep my delusions than pretend I'm a saint.
Better to concentrate on just being there
as I rinse a cup, untangle a snarl in your hair.

¶

Denatured time between self now and self then
cuts both ways: pity the stunned man with my face,
younger, wrapped tight in a marriage like razor ribbon,
dead drunk on the Merritt shoulder, out of gas.
Any way he moves, he's cut. He stares at the dim
green dash while back home his wife calls
and calls, and old lovers hang up, appalled.
My late twenties were a variation on this theme.
Gradually a frail light climbed out of the ocean,
I sobered up enough to walk. The days went on
without me. The woman's rage fell away. Nights
I worked alone, expecting nothing. As the blind
man's fingers are not blind, I saw with my heart's
vision: you, your mother. You would come in time.

TEXT AND COVER DESIGN BY TREE SWENSON.

COVER PHOTOGRAPH BY DUANE MICHALS
"THE ILLUMINATED MAN," 1969,
COURTESY SIDNEY JANIS GALLERY,
NEW YORK

TEXT TYPE IS FAIRFIELD WITH MERIDIEN
DISPLAY. COMPOSITION BY TYPEWORKS

MANUFACTURED BY EDWARDS BROTHERS

Library of Congress Cataloging-in-Publication Data

Skinner, Jeffrey.
A guide to forgetting.

(The National poetry series)
I. Gallagher, Tess. II. Title.
PS3569.K498G85 1988 811'.54 87-83085
ISBN 1-55597-108-3